MW01125594

Hey Kids! Let's Visit Philadelphia

Fun, Facts, and Amazing Discoveries for Kids

Teresa Mills

Life Experiences Publishing

Contents

Welcome

Philadelphia is a major United States city filled with parks, historical landmarks, museums, restaurants, shopping centers, universities, and many fun things to do. You will find tours, sports, history, and so much more! I love talking about history, so we will stroll through Philly from a historical perspective, learning about some of the famous places that shaped the United States and some of the more modern parks, tours, and places to visit!

This book is written as a fun fact guide about some attractions and sites in Philadelphia. It includes some history interspersed with fun facts about things to do. The book can easily be enjoyed by younger children through reading it with them. You can visit Philadelphia right from your own home! Whether you are preparing for a vacation with the family and want to learn more about the city or just want to learn a little more about the City of Brotherly Love, this book is for you.

As you continue to learn more about Philadelphia, I have some fun activity and coloring pages that you can download and print at:

https://kid-friendly-family-vacations.com/phillyfun

When you have completed this book, I invite you to visit the other books in the series:

Hey Kids! Let's Visit Washington DC
Hey Kids! Let's Visit A Cruise Ship
Hey Kids! Let's Visit New York City
Hey Kids! Let's Visit London England
Hey Kids! Let's Visit San Francisco
Hey Kids! Let's Visit Savannah Georgia
Hey Kids! Let's Visit Paris France
Hey Kids! Let's Visit Charleston South Carolina
Hey Kids! Let's Visit Chicago
Hey Kids! Let's Visit Rome Italy
Hey Kids! Let's Visit Boston
Hey Kids! Let's Visit Philadelphia
Hey Kids! Let's Visit San Diego
Hey Kids! Let's Visit Seattle
Hey Kids! Let's Visit Seoul South Korea

Enjoy!

Teresa Mills

A Little About Philadelphia

Philadelphia, known as the City of Brotherly Love, served as the capital of the United States until 1800. It is a city that is full of history – one of the most historical that you can visit, in fact. Philadelphia was founded in 1682. William Penn, an English Quaker, founded it as the capitol of the Pennsylvania Colony. William Penn received the land as a part of a land grant from King Charles II of England.

Philadelphia became a city in 1701 when William Penn issued the Charter of 1701. This charter, also called the Pennsylvania Charter of Privileges, granted the citizens a number of basic freedoms such as the freedom of worship. It also gave the colony the right to appoint leaders and make their own laws. The charter established Philadelphia as a city, and it continued to grow into an important center of trade by the 1750s. One leading citizen, Benjamin Franklin, helped improve services in the city and even established new services such as a hospital, a library, and a fire department. At this point in time, Philadelphia passed Boston as the busiest port and largest city in British America.

Philadelphia played an important role in the American Revolution and the independence of the United States. It was a meeting place for the founding fathers of America, including where the first Continental Congress met after the Boston Tea Party. The Declaration of Independence was signed in Philadelphia (1776) and the US Constitution was ratified (1788) there as well. Philadelphia served as the United States first capital from May 10, 1775, through December 12, 1776, and later from 1790-1800 while the capital in Washington DC was under construction.

Philadelphia also served as the capital of Pennsylvania until 1799 when it was moved to Lancaster. In 1812, Harrisburg became the capital of Pennsylvania, but Philadelphia remained the largest city in the United States until late in the 18th century.

Firsts in Philadelphia

- First brick house in the U.S. – 1682 – Penn's House

- First U.S. almanac – 1685 – *America's Messenger*

- First U.S. library – 1731 – the Library Company of Philadelphia

- First U.S. hospital - 1751 – Pennsylvania Hospital

- First bell cast in the U.S. – 1753 – the Liberty Bell

- First 4th of July event – 1776

- First U.S. Convention – 1787 – Constitutional Convention, where the Constitution of the United States written and adopted

- First stock exchange – 1790 – Philadelphia Stock Exchange

- First U.S. mint – 1792

- First U.S. African American Church – 1794 – Mother Bethel A.M.E. Church

- First U.S. zoo – 1874 (chartered 1859) – Philadelphia Zoo

- First U.S. World's Fair – 1876

- First Thanksgiving Day Parade – 1919

- Oldest U.S. street continuously occupied – 1713 – Elfreth's Alley

Today, Philadelphia is a major United States city with a passion for its past!

Are you ready? Let's Visit Philadelphia!

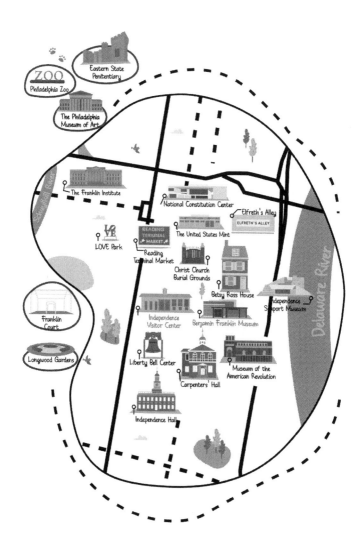

Map of Philadelphia Attractions

Chapter 1

Independence Visitor Center

The Independence Visitor Center should be your first stop on a historical tour of Philadelphia. This visitor center is where you will be able to learn more about the things to see in the historic district. This is the official visitor center of the Independence National Historical Park and is located at 1 N. Independence Mall W. in Philadelphia.

To help get you used to being in the historic area of Philadelphia, you will be able to see and interact with historical characters from the revolutionary era. There is also an exhibit that gives a little more information about Philadelphia's importance in American history.

Throughout the historic district of Philadelphia, there are 13 storytelling benches with trained storytellers sharing five-minute stories about the history of

Philadelphia. One set of storytelling benches is located in the visitor center.

Independence Visitor Center

Fun Facts About Philadelphia

- Philadelphia is sometimes called the City of Murals because there are over 3,800 murals in the city.

- The world's first computer was built at the University of Philadelphia in 1946. It was called the Electronic Numerical Integrator And Computer (ENIAC).

- Most people who live in Philadelphia love pretzels. They eat more than 12 times the number of pretzels per year than the average American.

Chapter 2

Liberty Bell Center

The Liberty Bell Center is located on Independence Mall in Philadelphia and is a part of the U.S. National Park Service as well as Independence National Historical Park. The center is located across from the visitor center and is free to visit.

The Liberty Bell was originally named the State House Bell because it was placed in the steeple of Pennsylvania's State House (which is now Independence Hall). The bell is a very iconic symbol of America's independence. It was ordered by the Pennsylvania Assembly in 1751 to commemorate the 50th anniversary of William Penn's Charter of Privileges (the Charter of 1701, which was the start of the Constitution of Pennsylvania).

The original bell was cast by the Whitechapel Bell Foundry of London in 1752. This bell proved to be very brittle and cracked upon its first ringing after arriving in

Philadelphia. Two local workmen, John Pass and John Stow, then recast the bell. The names Pass and Stow now appear on the bell.

The large crack that you see on the bell today is widely agreed upon to have happened in 1846. The bell had been used for 90 years prior to this and possibly developed hairline fractures through use. The city of Philadelphia wanted to repair the small cracks in the bell prior to George Washington's birthday in 1846. The repairs to the bell included some drilling to expand the cracks in order to keep the cracks from spreading. It turns out the repair was not successful as another crack appeared in the bell. This second crack is the one that silenced the bell forever.

The bell is cast with the words "Proclaim LIBERTY Throughout all the Land unto all the Inhabitants Thereof" which is a reference from Leviticus 25:10 in the Bible.

This is cast on the Liberty Bell:

Proclaim LIBERTY Throughout all the Land unto all the Inhabitants Thereof Lev. XXV. v X. By Order of the ASSEMBLY of the Province of PENSYLVANIA for the State House in Philad[A]

Pass and Stow

Philad^A MDCCLIII

The Liberty Bell

Note the different spelling of Pennsylvania on the bell (PENSYLVANIA). This is the spelling of Pennsylvania that was used in the first constitution of the state.

Fun Facts About the Liberty Bell

- The bell was not known as the Liberty Bell until the 1800s.

- When cast by Pass and Stow, the Liberty Bell weighed 2,080 pounds (943.5 kg).

- The Liberty Bell was first displayed outside of Philadelphia in 1884 at an exposition in New Orleans. It was displayed at other world's fairs and expositions during the late 19th and early 20th centuries.

Chapter 3

Independence Hall

Independence Hall is a part of Independence Square in the historic district of Philadelphia. Independence Hall was where both the U.S. Constitution (1787-1788) and the U.S. Declaration of Independence (1776) were debated and adopted by the U.S. founding fathers. The building that houses Independence Hall was originally built in 1753 and called the Pennsylvania State House at that time. This building can literally be defined as the Birthplace of America! Independence Hall is located at 520 Chestnut Street.

The State House served as the first capital of both the Commonwealth of Pennsylvania and of the United States of America. It was the main meeting place of the Second Continental Congress (1775-1781) as well as the site of the Constitutional Convention (1788).

Independence Hall

The building is made of red brick in a Georgian style. It has one main building with a belltower and two smaller wings on each side. The side wings and the steeple were constructed in 1781, much later than the original construction. The lowest chamber of the first wooden steeple was the first home of the Liberty Bell.

Visitors to Independence Hall will be able to see the Assembly Room on the first floor of the building. This is the room where the Constitution and the Declaration of Independence were both signed.

Fun Facts About Independence Hall

- The Liberty Bell was originally crafted for the State House (now Independence Hall).

- In the Hall, you can see an original copy of the U.S. Constitution and the inkwell that was used by signers of the Declaration of Independence.

- The Liberty Bell was hanging in the State House in 1776 and was rung (or believed to have rung) to help celebrate the first public reading of the U.S. Declaration of Independence on July 8, 1776.

Chapter 4

Congress Hall

Congress Hall, originally the Philadelphia Courthouse (constructed 1787-1789), housed the U.S. Congress from 1790 through 1800. Philadelphia was the temporary capital of the United States at that time. The building is a two-story brick building located at the corner of Chestnut and 6th streets (600 Chestnut St.) in Philadelphia and is a part of the Independence National Historical Park. Congress Hall is actually conjoined with Independence Hall right next door!

When the Congress Hall was in use, the House of Representatives met on the first floor while the Senate met on the second floor. Some other cool historical happenings at the Hall include the second inauguration of George Washington, the inauguration of John Adams, the start of the U.S. mint, the creation of the First Bank of the United States, and the creation of the Department of the Navy.

Congress Hall

The Congress Hall building is now managed by the
National Park Service. It was restored to its 1796
appearance during the 20th century and is open for
tours daily. The tours are led by National Park Rangers.

Fun Facts About Congress Hall

- The Bill of Rights of the U.S. Constitution was ratified in Congress Hall on December 15, 1791.

- After the capital of the United States moved to Washington D.C., the building continued to serve as the Philadelphia Courthouse.

- The large second floor back room, which was called the Common Council Chamber, was the home to the U.S. Supreme Court from 1791-1800.

Chapter 5

Christ Church and Burial Ground

Christ Church in Old City Philadelphia was founded in 1695 and is located at 20 N. American St. in Philadelphia. It was originally founded as a parish of the Church of England, and then it played an important role in the start of the Protestant Episcopal Church in the U.S. From 1754 to 1810, the tower and steeple of the church was the tallest structure in all of the thirteen colonies at 196 ft (60 m).

In the early days, the congregation of the church included 15 signers of the Declaration of Independence. There were also American Revolutionary War leaders who attended the church including Betsy Ross, Benjamin Franklin, Robert Morris, and George Washington. If you visit the church, there are plaques marking the pews where these leaders regularly sat during worship.

Christ Church is an active Episcopal Church in Philadelphia, still holding weekly services. Visitors can tour the church and listen to some of the 300+ year history and learn the roles that the church played during the American Revolution.

Christ Church in Old City Philadelphia

The Christ Church Burial Ground is located at the intersection of Arch and 5th Streets and was established in 1719. Before 1719, earlier members of the church were buried in the churchyard, which was a common practice during that time. The Arch and 5th Street location was used after the churchyard burial grounds were full.

The later Burial Ground is the final resting place for more than 4,000 members of Christ Church. Among those were five signers of the Declaration of Independence including Dr. Benjamin Rush, George Ross, Frances Hopkinson, Joseph Hewes, and Benjamin Franklin. Many other military heroes, lawyers, early leaders of the nation, and some victims of the Yellow Fever epidemic of 1793.

One of the most famous gravesites in the Burial Ground is of Benjamin Franklin and his family. Benjamin Franklin passed away in 1790 and is buried in a family plot in the Christ Church Burial Ground. The Benjamin Franklin burial plot is marked with a marble ledger tablet. A tradition of tossing pennies onto the gravesite is said to be in respect to one of Franklin's most famous quotes: "A penny saved is a penny earned."

Benjamin Franklin Family Burial Site

Facts About Christ Church and Burial Ground

- In honor of Benjamin Franklin's 300th birthday in 2005, the Christ Church Preservation Trust had a brick path built around the Benjamin Franklin family burial site.

- Benjamin Franklin's grave site can still be viewed through a set of iron rails even when the burial ground is closed.

- Christ Church is registered as a national Historic Landmark. More than 250,000 people visit the church each year while more than 100,000 visit the burial ground each year.

Chapter 6

Betsy Ross House

The Betsy Ross House is located at 239 Arch St. in Philadelphia. It is traditionally known as the place where Betsy sewed the first flag of the United States of America in May of 1776. Historians are not in full agreement that Betsy actually lived in this house, but it serves as the landmark for honoring her and the first flag. Betsy would have lived in the house from approximately 1773-1785, which was the same time period that the flag was designed.

The house is a few blocks from the Liberty Bell and Independence Hall and is very close to Christ Church. Betsy worshiped at Christ Church.

When visiting the house, you will find "Betsy Ross" in the upholstery shop. The character will explain a little about her life as an upholsterer and seamstress.

Betsy Ross House

The role of Betsy and her place in history does not have a lot of documented evidence as most of the history has been passed down through her family. But the Pennsylvania Historical and Museum Commission placed a plaque at the house in 2009 recognizing her contribution to American History.

Betsy Ross was a skilled upholsterer (an artist who covers furniture frames with fabric or leather and padding for making beds, chairs, mattresses, sofas, etc.) and flag maker. She is credited with the use of the five-pointed star in the American flag. One of the first designs used a six-pointed star. Betsy made flags for the state of Pennsylvania and the United States of America for over 50 years.

The Betsy Ross Flag (as the first United States flag has become known) has 13 alternating red and white stripes and a blue patch in the upper left corner with 13 five-pointed stars in a circle. The flag was requested by General George Washington along with the Continental Congress to signify a new nation. The Betsy Ross flag is known as the original American flag. The 13 stripes and 13 stars represent the original 13 colonies.

The Betsy Ross Flag

Fun Facts About Betsy Ross, the House, and the Betsy Ross Flag

- Betsy was married and widowed three times – twice before the age of thirty. She is known as a symbol of perseverance through tragedy as she succeeded as an entrepreneur running her seamstress business to help raise her seven children.

- At the Betsy Ross House, there is an exhibit that talks about the jobs and contributions of women in Colonial America.

- The 13 stars on the flag are in a circle to represent that no one colony would be viewed as more important than another.

Chapter 7

Elfreth's Alley

Elfreth's Alley dates back to 1703 and is located between North Front Street and North 2nd Street in Philadelphia. The 32 houses that are on this street were built between the 1720s and 1830s, and it has the honor of being the oldest street in America. The alley is named for property owner and blacksmith Jeremiah Elfreth and was home to tradespeople and artisans in colonial Philadelphia.

During colonial times, most businesses were operated out of people's homes. On this alley in the 18th century, you would have found shoemakers, cabinet makers, grocers, glassblowers, tailors, and others. What is unique about the alley is that even in today's modern times, this alley has been preserved as it was three centuries ago, and it is a bustling residential alley as well. Elfreth's Alley is considered to be the oldest continuously inhabited street in the U.S.

Elfreth's Alley

Two of the homes on Elfreth's Alley, #124 and #126, are open as a gift shop and a museum that can be toured. In this museum home, you will be able to learn about some of the many artisans who may have lived and worked in the alley during the 18th century as well as some history of the alley.

The homes in the city center were owned by prosperous merchants and landowners. The working middle class lived in the smaller neighborhoods to the north by the Delaware river, such as Elfreth's Alley.

Fun Facts about Elfreth's Alley

- Though the alley homes in the 18th century were used as both homes and businesses, by the 19th century the homes were used simply as family homes. In the 19th century, up to 8 families would share two homes. That is up to 27 people sharing two small homes.

- On the first Saturday in December, the residents open their doors to the public for an event called "Deck the Alley." Here you will see the homes decorated for the holidays, hear carolers and musicians, and can try baked goods and cider – all to celebrate the season.

- In June of each year, an event called Fete Day is held, which dates back to 1934. On Fete Day, the residents open their homes to show what 21st century life looks like in Elfreth's Alley.

Chapter 8

Franklin Court

Franklin Court, located between Chestnut and Market Streets and 3rd and 4th Streets in the Independence National Historic Park, is the site of Benjamin Franklin's brick home. Franklin and his family lived here while he served in the Continental Congress and the Constitutional Convention. Benjamin Franklin owned the home until he died in 1790. The location of the house is represented by what are called "ghost structures" – steel structures that outline where a building used to stand. The firm of Venturi and Rauch designed the Franklin Court Complex, and it was opened in 1976 – just in time for the Bicentennial Celebration of the United States.

Franklin's house was large for the time. It was three stories tall and had 10 rooms. For the 18th century, it could be considered a mansion. Since there were no real records of what the house looked like before it was torn down in 1812, the architect firm decided to build a ghost structure where the house once stood instead of building a reconstruction. You can look through the structure to see the house's foundation, wells, and privy (toilet) pits.

Benjamin Franklin

Also in Franklin Court, you will find the Benjamin Franklin Museum, a working 18th century printing office reproduction, an operating post office, and other exhibits. The Benjamin Franklin Museum is an underground museum that houses paintings and replicas of some of Franklin's inventions such as a glass harmonica, the Franklin stove, and a swim fin. The U.S. Postal Service Museum has exhibits of Franklin's Pennsylvania Gazette and Pony Express pouches. The printing office has displays of demonstrations of 18th century printing and binding.

When the Franklin's house was being built, Franklin's wife Deborah was the one who oversaw the construction. Benjamin was in London during the entire construction, sending specific instructions about the work in letters that he sent. There are excerpts of these letters on display throughout the court. Franklin and his wife never lived in the house together as Deborah died from the effects of a stroke in 1774. In the five years before his death in 1790, Franklin made several renovations to the house including adding the bindery (a factory or workshop where book pages are put together with a cover to form the book), printing shop, and foundry (a factory or workshop where melted metal is cast in molds) for his grandson. He also added a wing onto the house that had a dining room, additional bedrooms, and a library.

Fun Facts About Benjamin Franklin

- Benjamin Franklin was multi-talented. He was an author, a publisher, an inventor, a printer, a diplomat, a statesman, a Postmaster, and more.

- Franklin founded the Pennsylvania Hospital, the University of Pennsylvania, the Library Company, and the American Philosophical Society.

- In June of 1776, Franklin was appointed to the Committee of Five (a group of five members of the Second Continental Congress) who drafted the Declaration of Independence.

- Franklin proved that lightning is "electricity" by flying a kite in a thunderstorm on June 15, 1752, possibly in Philadelphia. He wrote about it in the Pennsylvania Gazette on October 19, 1752, but never actually said whether he performed the experiment himself. The experiment was originally tried by Thomas-Francois Dalibard in France on May 10 of that same year.

Chapter 9

Carpenters' Hall

Carpenters' Hall, located at 320 Chestnut Street, is also a part of the Independence National Historic Park. It is a two-story brick building that was used as a meeting hall. The building had just been completed when it played host to the First Continental Congress, which met from September 5-October 26, 1774, in response to the Intolerable Acts. This act by the British closed off the Boston Port and overturned the Massachusetts Charter, basically bringing the colony of Massachusetts under British control a little more.

Carpenters' Hall was designed by Robert Smith, a master builder and member of the Carpenters' Company. Carpenters' Hall was built as the headquarters for the Carpenters' Company. The company was founded in 1724 to share information about the art of building, to help determine the value of completed work, and to help architects sharpen their skills. The Carpenters' Company held regular meetings as a trade guild (an association of craftsmen or merchants) for over 275 years.

Carpenters' Hall

The location of Carpenters' Hall in the hub of Colonial Philadelphia made it easy for the members to be in the center of political activity, thus being a great location for the First Continental Congress. In addition to political events, the building also was home to other businesses over the years. In 1791, it served as the headquarters of the First Bank of the United States. Other businesses to be located in the building were the U.S. Customs House, the Bank of the State of Pennsylvania, the Franklin Institute, the Society of Friends (the Quakers – a Christian group that started in England), the Philadelphia Auction Market, and several others.

If you visit Carpenters' Hall, you will see the eight Windsor chairs that were used by the members of the First Continental Congress.

Fun Facts About Carpenters' Hall

- The First Continental Congress attendees included Patrick Henry, John Adams, Samuel Adams, and George Washington.

- The building is fascinating to tour as it was built by craftsmen for craftsmen. The design and features of the building are said to be an almost flawless example of Georgian architecture (a style of architecture that was popular from 1700-1830 and was named for the reigns of the first four King Georges of England).

- Carpenters' Hall is still privately owned and operated by the Carpenters' Company and is free to enter and tour.

Chapter 10

National Constitution Center

The National Constitution Center can be found at 525 Arch Street. It is a 160,000 square foot (14,864 square meter) museum and media center dedicated to the Constitution of the United States of America. This center will help you explore the U.S. Constitution through interactive displays, artifacts, and high-tech exhibits.

Inside the museum, a few of the things that you will be able to see and participate in are:

- An original copy of Abraham Lincoln's Emancipation Proclamation — a document which declared "that all persons held as slaves are, and henceforward shall be free."

- A surviving copy of the original Bill of Rights –
the first 10 amendments to the U.S. Constitution.
These were written by James Madison.

- Signers' Hall – a gallery where you can
pose with bronze statues of the Founding
Fathers (42 revolutionaries who signed the U.S.
Constitution).

- The American National Tree – an interactive
exhibit that sheds light on close to 100 citizens
who left an impact on the country.

- The 19th Amendment: How Women Won the
Vote – an exhibit where you can learn of
the struggles and triumphs surrounding women
earning the right to vote in the U.S.

- Freedom Rising theater program – a live
performance that Justice Sandra Day O'Conner
called "the best 17-minute civics lesson."

Preamble of the Constitution on the National Constitution Center building

Fun Facts About the U.S. Constitution

- The U.S. Constitution contains only 4,400 words, making it the shortest written Constitution of any major government in the world.

- The formal term "The United States of America" was used for the first time in the U.S. Constitution.

- Benjamin Franklin was the oldest citizen to sign the U.S. Constitution. He was 81 at the time. His health was poor at that time, and he needed help signing. It is said that tears were streaming down his face as he signed.

Chapter 11

The United States Mint in Philadelphia

The Philadelphia Mint is the nation's first mint. It is located at 151 N Independence Mall E and was originally opened in 1792. Currently, the Philadelphia Mint produces coin and medal dies (sort of like molds). Items minted in Philadelphia include:

- Circulating coins

- Annual uncirculated coin sets

- Commemorative coins

- Medals

Coins for the United States have been minted in
Philadelphia for over two centuries. There are two
additional mints in the United States – in San Francisco
and Denver – but at least half of the circulating coins
(coins that are in use for making purchases) are minted
in Philadelphia. If a coin is minted in Philadelphia, it
will have a "P" stamped on it. The U.S. dime below was
minted in Philadelphia.

United States dime minted in Philadelphia

The original building (the one built in 1792) was located
at 7th and Arch streets – about two blocks from
the current location on Independence Mall East. The
current building is actually the fourth building to house
the Philadelphia Mint. The current building opened
in 1969 and was designed by Philadelphia architect
Vincent G. Kling. This mint has the Tiffany glass mosaics
from the third mint building installed.

The Philadelphia Mint

Fun Facts About the Philadelphia Mint

- The mint can produce close to one million coins in 30 minutes.

- There is a stuffed bird in the lobby of the Philadelphia Mint. Before he died, he was allowed to fly around the coins for good luck.

- On a tour of the mint, you will see the operations floor. There are also interactive displays that show many of the commemorative coin designs that were minted in Philadelphia.

Chapter 12

Museum of the American Revolution

The Museum of the American Revolution can be found at 101 S. Third Street in the Philadelphia Historic District. It is a museum that is dedicated to telling the story of the American Revolution. The museum houses several thousand objects including books, manuscripts, weapons, artwork, and sculptures displayed in galleries. In addition, there are films and rotating exhibits that make learning about the revolution more exciting.

A three-story building houses the museum. The first floor of the museum has a shop, a cafe, a theater, and an exhibit gallery. The second floor has a series of galleries and a theater that is dedicated to the exhibit of George Washington's marquee tent (his headquarters tent) that was used during the war for independence. The tent is a part of a multimedia presentation about George Washington. The third floor has rooms for events.

The Museum of the American Revolution

Fun Facts About the Museum of the American Revolution

- George Washington required that the entire Continental Army be inoculated (vaccinated) against smallpox in the winter of 1777. He did this because disease, not combat, was one of the leading causes of death during the war.

- Women fought in the Continental Army. One of the most famous was Deborah Sampson. She disguised herself as a man (Robert Shurtleff) and fought for two years.

- Paul Revere was asked to use his hobby of dentistry to help identify a badly decomposed body of a fallen soldier.

- Invisible ink was used in the American Revolutionary War to communicate secret messages. The ink was created by Dr. James Jay and was made from ferrous sulfate and water. The ink was used to write messages between the lines of letters or in books. To reveal the hidden message, the page was held over a heat source or wet with a revealing chemical.

Chapter 13

The Independence Seaport Museum

The Independence Seaport Museum is located in Penn's Landing along the Delaware River. Penn's Landing is a waterfront area created to commemorate the landing of William Penn in 1682. The landing has several historic ships docked on the pier and has a space for outdoor events that are usually held during the summer. The museum has one of the largest collections of maritime exhibits, boats, and models in North America.

Some of the things that you will see and be able to interact with at the Seaport Museum are:

- A traditional boat shop, the workshop on the water – a working boat shop where you can interact with wooden boat builders. The boat shop is dedicated to the tradition of wooden boat building and sailing. The shop helps maintain the museum's collection of boats as well as restores boats owned by others.

- The Cruiser Olympia and the unknown soldier – the cruiser Olympia was the ship chosen to transport the casket of the unknown soldier who is laid to rest in the Tomb of the Unknown Soldier in Arlington National Cemetery in Washington DC. On the cruiser, you will see the marker that is in place to mark where the casket was laid during the journey from Le Harve, France, to the Washington Navy Yard. The Olympia left France on October 25, 1921, and arrived at the Washington Navy Yard on November 9, 1921.

- The J. Welles Henderson Research Center – a research center with one of the largest collections of regional maritime research in the U.S. (regional to the Delaware River, and ports of Camden, Wilmington, and Philadelphia).

- Submarine Becuna – you can tour the submarine that launched on January 30, 1944, and was commissioned on May 27, 1944. This submarine was instrumental in World War II.

- The River Alive Exhibit – this exhibit was built to help visitors learn the importance of keeping our waterways clean.

- The Patriots and Pirates Exhibit – this exhibit

helps visitors understand about the U.S. Navy's conflicts with pirates during the late 1700s and early 1800s. You can climb aboard the Schooner Diligence to learn a little more about the type of ships that played a role in protecting merchant ships from pirates.

- The Tides of Freedom Exhibit – an exhibit celebrating the African presence on the Delaware River.

The Cruiser Olympia

Fun Facts About the Independence Seaport Museum

- The giant pirate ship – the Schooner Diligence – in the Patriots and Pirates Exhibit is a place for kids to climb, steer the ship, and raise and lower the sail.

- Kids and adults can rent museum-built rowboats to enjoy the waterways around the museum.

- The museum offers a summer camp to explore the history of Philadelphia's waterways. This camp is available to campers ages 6-12.

Chapter 14

The Franklin Institute

The Franklin Institute is a science museum as well as a center for science education. This museum is named for Benjamin Franklin, an American scientist and statesman who was also a Philadelphia resident. The Institute is one of the oldest centers for science development and education in the United States. The museum is located at 222 N. 20th Street in Philadelphia and holds the honor of being Pennsylvania's most visited museum.

The Franklin Institute

Some of the fascinating things you will find at the
Franklin Institute are:

- The Fels Planetarium – a variety of astronomical
  presentations are played on a 60-foot
  (18.3-meter) diameter giant dome.

- The Benjamin Franklin Memorial – in the
  rotunda of the museum sits a 20-foot (6.1-meter)
  tall marble statue of Benjamin Franklin. The
  memorial offers a multimedia show that explains
  the impact that Benjamin Franklin had on the
  world. Franklin was a statesman, a civic leader,
  and scientist.

- An outdoor science park that offers a place for
  families to re-charge.

- Holt and Miller Observatory – an area with a 10-foot (3-meter) telescope that allows you to safely view the sun and offers a cool view of the Philadelphia Skyline.

- The Giant Heart Exhibit – a walkthrough experience with a two-story replica of a human heart. Walk through to get an understanding of the operation of the heart.

- The Electricity Exhibit – here you can witness lightning up close, feel a static charge, use your body to complete an electric circuit, and see Benjamin Franklin's Lightning Rod.

- The Your Brain Exhibit – follow through different exhibits to learn about the brain and the brain's functions. Climb through neural networks, scan a brain, and learn how neurons fire.

- The Franklin Air Show Exhibit – put your piloting skills to work! You will see artifacts from the Wright Brothers, play with airplane controls in pilot training, and participate in an activity to test your wings as you attempt a take-off.

And several other exhibits.

Fun Facts About the Franklin Institute

- Benjamin Franklin's glass "armonica", a musical instrument he invented, can be seen at the institute.

- The statue of Benjamin Franklin in the rotunda weighs 30 tons (27,216 kg) and is sitting up on a pedestal that weighs 92 tons (83,461 kg).

- The sounds of the heartbeat can be heard as you walk through the giant heart exhibit.

Chapter 15

The Philadelphia Museum of Art

The Philadelphia Museum of Art can be found at 2600 Benjamin Franklin Parkway and is one of the largest art museums in the country. It houses pieces of art from medieval times, impressionist times, the Renaissance, the ancient world, and modern times. It has a wide variety of pieces of artwork, including suits of armor, famous paintings, and an outdoor sculpture garden.

Some of the things that are located in the museum are:

- Grace Kelly's wedding gown

- Artworks depicting Benjamin Franklin – cups, medallions, plates, vases, portraits, etc.

- Artwork by Philadelphia's contemporary artists

- Different varieties of masks – helmets, ceremonial masks, defense helmets, and defense visors

- Paintings, drawings, and other works of art

- An outdoor sculpture garden

And much more.

The Rocky Steps

The Rocky movies that were filmed and popular in the 1970s, 80s, and 90s along with sequels in the early 2000s show the films' star Rocky Balboa's run up the eastern entrance steps. The museum steps are affectionately called "The Rocky Steps." Some film critics say that the Rocky Steps are the second most famous movie location after Grand Central Station.

The bronze Rocky statue that is 8.5 feet (2.6 meters) tall was commissioned and used in the filming of Rocky III in 1982. For that filming, the statue was placed at the top of the steps. Later, it was placed in a permanent display area at the bottom of the steps of the art museum.

The museum steps and the Rocky statue are some of the most famous tourist attractions in the city of Philadelphia. People can be seen recreating the scene from the movies by running up the 72 museum steps and having a photo taken with the famous statue.

The Philadelphia Museum of Art

Fun Facts About the Museum and the Rocky Steps

- The museum houses over 240,000 works of art that span over 4,000 years.

- The museum opened its doors to the public in 1928.

- The museum covers more than 1,000,000 square feet (92,903 square meters) of space, which includes the main building, the Ruth and Raymond G. Perelman Building, the Mount Pleasant and Cedar Grove Park Houses, and the Rodin Museum.

The Rocky Statue

Chapter 16

Fairmount Park

Fairmount Park is the largest city (municipal) park in Philadelphia. It consists of two different sections, East Park and West Park. The two park sections are divided by the Schuylkill River. The two sections together cover a total of 2,052 acres.

The park is Philadelphia's first park. The Philadelphia Zoo is located in West Park. Just across the river in East Park, the Philadelphia Museum of Art is at the headway of the park. The park continues north along both sides of the river. Among the many attractions and things to do at the park are:

- The Shofuso Japanese House and Garden – located in the western section of the park, it is a traditional style Japanese house and reflects the history of Japanese culture in Philadelphia.

- Strawberry Mansion – in East Park, a mansion built by Judge William Lewis in 1789 as a summer home. Judge Lewis was an advisor to Alexander Hamilton and George Washington.

- Fairmount Water Works – this was once the home of the engine room of Philly's water department and is now a National Historic Landmark. From here you can see Boathouse Row and the Philadelphia Museum of Art.

- Boathouse Row – in East Park, a row of 19th century boathouses. At night, lights outline the row for a beautiful view.

- Miles and miles of trails, both wooded and natural.

- Mansions throughout the park where the elite used to spend summers.

- Fairmount Park Horticulture Center – this area in West Park has manicured lawns and a greenhouse for your enjoyment.

- Mann Center – in West Park, A-list musicians make their way to Mann Center for summer tours.

- Laurel Hill Cemetery – in East Park, a final resting place for some Titanic passengers, Civil War era generals, and other notable Philadelphia residents.

- Smith Memorial Playground – in East Park,

this playground built in the 1800s sports a 1600 square foot (148.6 square meter) playhouse, jungle gyms, and a giant wooden slide.

- Zipline at Treetop Quest Philly – in West Park, an aerial adventure park.

- Touch everything at the Pease Touch Museum – in Memorial Hall in West Park, this is a play-centric educational place where kids can touch everything.

Walking Trails at Fairmount Park

Fun Facts About Fairmount Park

- There are 152 sculptures in Fairmount Park. The first sculpture was Night, a bronze statue near the Horticulture Center that was purchased in 1872.

- There are 16 creeks that run through Fairmount Park.

- There is a 3.8-mile (6.12-km) gravel and dirt path in the park called Boxer's Trail. It is named this because Philadelphia boxer "Smokin" Joe Frazier trained there.

Chapter 17

Reading Terminal Market

The Reading Terminal Market is located at 12th and Arch Streets in the center of Philadelphia and is one of the oldest public markets in America. It was first opened in 1893 under the elevated train shed. As a little history, markets in Philadelphia were originally set up on High Street along the Delaware River. This original market was called the "Jersey Market" (most of the merchants were from New Jersey). In 1859, through concerns about health and safety, street markets were dismantled. Then two main markets were formed, The Farmer's Market and Franklin Market. These two markets were the beginnings of what would become the Reading Terminal Market.

When the Reading Terminal Market opened in 1893, there was approximately 78,000 square feet (7,246 square meters) of space for almost 800 merchants in 6-foot stalls. The market was a state-of-the-art facility that had a refrigeration system with a half million cubic feet and 52 rooms. The market even later offered a basket delivery system on suburban trains: a homeowner would place a grocery order that would be filled at the market and then placed on the train to their town. The basket was then held at the train station and picked up by the homeowner.

During the Great Depression of the 1930s, the Reading Terminal Market prospered mainly because local farmers were very eager to bring their goods to the market to sell. In addition, during World War II, local farmers were eager to sell their goods in the market. However, by the 1960s, the market fell into disrepair due to lack of funding for the railroads. The railroad company fell into bankruptcy in 1971. Ultimately, the market ceased to exist in 1976.

In the early 1990s, thanks to the reawakening of the Philadelphia commercial center, construction was started to revitalize the market. Today, there are now more than 80 merchants set up in the market. Cooks from Philadelphia's local restaurants come through the market each day for the freshest produce and hard to find ingredients, so this is a very lively and active market.

Produce in the Reading Terminal Market

Fun Facts About The Reading Terminal Market

- Two of the merchants that operate in the Reading Terminal Market are descendants of the original owners.

- In addition to a huge food bazaar, you can also buy crafts, quilts, flowers, and just about anything you can imagine at the market.

- The northwestern corner of the market is mainly occupied by Amish merchants from Lancaster County, Pennsylvania. At the market, you can see Amish bakers twisting and baking soft pretzels.

Chapter 18

LOVE Park and Sculpture

LOVE Park, located at 16th and JFK Boulevard, is the better-known name of Philadelphia's John F. Kennedy Plaza. LOVE park is the passage between City Hall and places like the Franklin Institute and the Philadelphia Museum of Art, a sort of grand entrance to Benjamin Franklin Parkway. LOVE Park was built in 1965 and dedicated as John F. Kennedy Plaza in 1967.

Between 2016 and 2018, the park went through a major renovation project. The park was turned into a greener space that contains small lawns, two gardens, cafe seating, an open view of Benjamin Franklin Parkway, and daily recreational activities. It is a warm and welcoming park where you will often see people having lunch, sunbathers, people jogging, and performers. A beautifully re-designed fountain is located in a large oval paved area. The fountain has a large jet with smaller programmable light up jets surrounding it.

The LOVE Sculpture was designed by Robert Indiana and has been in LOVE Park since 1976. It was placed there in 1976 as a part of the U.S. Bicentennial. It was briefly removed from the park in 1978 but was then purchased by a Philadelphia businessman and replaced in the park. During the 2016-2018 renovation of the park, the sculpture was once again returned with a fresh coat of paint.

LOVE Sculpture

Fun Facts About LOVE Park and Sculpture

- If you are visiting LOVE Park on a Wednesday, you may see a wedding taking place under the iconic LOVE Sculpture. Couples can register in advance to have their wedding there on a Wednesday between March and October.

- In November and December, LOVE Park hosts Philadelphia's annual Christmas Village. You will find vendors selling handmade crafts, small gifts, and snacks in the open-air market.

- On weekdays between 11 am and 3 pm, you will find a rotating food truck line-up.

Chapter 19

Philadelphia Zoo

The Philadelphia Zoo has the honor of being the first and oldest and zoo in the U.S. It was chartered in 1859, opened in 1874 due to the U.S. Civil War. Just like Philadelphia has many "firsts," the zoo in Philadelphia can also boast many firsts:

- The first births of orangutans and chimps in a U.S. zoo – 1928

- The first cheetahs born in a zoo – 1956

- The first children's zoo – 1957

- The first birth of an echidna (a spiny anteater) in North America – 1983

- The first white lion exhibit – 1993

- The first birth of a giant river otter in North America – 2004

Giraffes in the Philadelphia Zoo

A unique trail feature at the Philadelphia Zoo is Zoo360 – an animal exploration trail experience. This system gives the animals more freedom to move around the zoo grounds and even above the zoo grounds. As you explore and move around the zoo, the zoo is actually moving around you at the same time. Zoo360 consists of five different trails within the zoo facility – Meerkat Maze, Great Ape Trail, Treetop Trail, Gorilla Treeway, and Big Cat Crossing.

In addition to all of the animals and Zoo360, some of the attractions at the zoo include:

- Hamilton Family KidZooU and Faris Family Education Center – a children's zoo offering petting opportunities with smaller animals.

- Small Mammal House – small mammal species like the dwarf mongoose, the Hoffman's two-toed sloth, the vampire bat, and meerkats to name a few.

- Penguin Point – home to 17 Humboldt penguins.

- Ride the Septa PZ Express Train

- WildWorks Ropes Course

Fun Facts About the Philadelphia Zoo

- The zoo first opened with 1,000 animals. The admission price in 1874 was 25 cents.

- The zoo is known for its architecture, which was the historic design of William Penn's grandson's country home.

- Big Cat Falls is home to tigers, pumas, jaguars, leopards, lions, and pumas. They live in an exhibit that has pools and waterfalls.

Chapter 20

Eastern State Penitentiary

The Eastern State Penitentiary is known as America's most historic prison. It opened in 1829 and was in use as a prison for 142 years, closing in 1971. Since its closing in 1971, the prison has been named a National Historic Landmark.

The prison redefined imprisonment by adopting a system of reform instead of punishment. This was done by separating the inmates into cells by themselves as a form of rehabilitation. This new system of imprisonment was called the "Pennsylvania system" or separate system. In this system, the prison warden was required to visit each inmate every day.

Eastern State Penitentiary

The layout of the prison was revolutionary when built. It was built with a wagon-wheel design with 7 wings of individual cells leading from a central hub. The prison had flush toilets, central heating, and showers in each private cell. Each inmate lived in complete isolation in this prison. The inmates were allowed to have a Bible as their only possession. They had daily chores such as weaving or shoemaking to occupy their time. In order to keep the prisoners completely isolated, they would exercise in an individual yard right outside their cell – again, completely separated.

Eventually, the state gave up trying to maintain this type of prison system in 1913. At that time, prisoners were allowed to share cells, work together, and even play in organized sports. This type of prison system was much easier to maintain. One of the main reasons for the change was the rapid growth of Pennsylvania. The prison was originally set up to house 300 inmates. By the 1920s, it housed over 2,000 inmates. Today, the prison operates as a historic site and museum.

Eastern State Penitentiary - Cell Block

Fun Facts About the Eastern State Penitentiary

- A couple of famous inmates at the prison were "Slick Willie" Sutton and "Scarface" Al Capone.

- Each year for Halloween, the prison is opened with five haunted houses set up as well as tours and live entertainment.

- The prison facility is maintained as a "preserved ruin." This means that no significant restoration or renovation was attempted. However, in 1991, some funds came available to preserve and stabilize the prison.

Chapter 21

Philly Cheesesteak

A Philly cheesesteak is basically a sandwich made from thin slices of steak (rib-eye or top round) and melted cheese (American, provolone, or Cheez Whiz) on a long hoagie roll. It is sometimes referred to as a Philadelphia cheesesteak, a cheesesteak, or steak and cheese (among other variations) and was originally created in Philadelphia. The invention of the cheesesteak is credited to Pat and Harry Olivieri. Pat would ultimately open a shop dedicated to the cheesesteak called Pat's King of Steaks, which is still in business in Philadelphia today.

Having a cheesesteak is almost as important when visiting Philadelphia as journeying through the Revolutionary History that is all around the town. There are a multitude of places to grab one of these iconic sandwiches including the original Pat's. Geno's is another cheesesteak mainstay, which popped up close to the same time that Pat's began serving cheesesteaks.

Philly Cheesesteak

There are many variations to the cheesesteak sandwich.
Common toppings are grilled or sauteed onions,
ketchup, and sweet or hot peppers.

Fun Facts About the Philly Cheesesteak Sandwich

- The original cheesesteak made by Pat and Harry did not have cheese on it.

- Pat's King of Steaks sells close to 6,000 Philly cheesesteaks in any weekend.

- In 1998, a 365-foot, 7-inch (112-meter) cheesesteak (stretched a little longer than a football field) was made by the Philadelphia Eagles. It weighed 1,790 pounds (812 kg) and was made on a single roll.

- In Philadelphia, you can get a cheesesteak 24 hours a day.

Chapter 22

Philadelphia Walking Tours

A great way to see and learn more about Philadelphia is to simply take a walking tour. Some of the companies that offer family friendly walking tours in Philly are:

The Constitutional Walking Tour

The Constitutional Walking Tour is a 75-minute, 1.25-mile (2-km) tour that gives an overview of the Independence National Historical Park area. The tour visits a lot of the historic sites in the birthplace of America, including the Liberty Bell and Independence Hall. The company runs tours from April through November, 7 days a week.

WeVenture Philadelphia Tours

WeVenture offers tours and experiences with local expert guides. They pride themselves on promoting local businesses, teaching respect for local residents, and contributing to communities. They offer a variety of walking tours including History, Highlights, & Revolution, a South Philly Art Tour, and a Rocky Movie Locations Tour. One of the most popular tours that WeVenture offers is the half-day American Revolution Tour in Valley Forge.

Intrepid Urban Adventures – Philadelphia

Intrepid Urban Adventures offers tours of Philadelphia from a local perspective. The company offers tour guides who will share information about the sites along with offbeat stories.

Chapter 23

Philadelphia Ghost Tours

Ghost tours are not for everyone, but if they are something you enjoy, it can be a great way to walk through the city and hear some great ghost stories too! The following companies offer family friendly ghost tours in Philadelphia.

Philadelphia Ghost Tour

Philadelphia Ghost Tour company offers ghost tours based on the book, *Ghost Stories of Philadelphia, PA.* The tours are offered nightly. Tours are candlelight-guided as you wander through the back streets of Philadelphia, Old City, and Independence National Park past haunted houses and graveyards.

Philly Ghosts

Philly Ghosts offers historic and entertaining walking ghost tours of the Old City of Philadelphia. A popular tour by Philly Ghosts is the "Phantoms of Philadelphia" tour – a spooky after dark ghost tour about some of the oldest residential neighborhoods in America. You will also see top Philadelphia landmarks such as the Liberty Bell, the First Bank of the United States, and Independence Hall.

Spirit of '76 Ghost Tour by City Tours

"Terrifying tales from Haunted Philadelphia" is the scary tagline form this tour. This is a 75-minute tour that visits 20 scary sites in Philadelphia's Old City. The guides will share stories by Edgar Allen Poe, who used to live in Philadelphia. The tour also covers some ghosts of legend who inhabit Carpenters' Hall and Independence Hall.

Chapter 24

Philadelphia Bike and Segway Tours

For the more adventurous at heart, what about a tour of Philly on a bike or a Segway? Biking is a great way to get out and move around; you will cover more ground than on a walking tour and get a little exercise. A Segway (a two-wheeled self-balancing personal transportation machine) tour can be even more adventurous! Both types of tours are available in Philadelphia. Here is a little more information.

Philly Bike Tour Co.

Philly Bike Tour Co. offers bike tours throughout Philadelphia in April-October, and tours are available November-March by contacting them for information. The tour company started touring with their Classic City Tour in 2013 and have been expanding their tours since. Still a favorite, the Classic City Tour is a 3.5-hour tour though the city to see the classic city sites. They cover 10 miles (16.1 km) and hit up about a dozen stops along the way. Some additional tours are the Fairmount Park Story tour and the Murals & Public Art tour. Private and custom tours are available.

Philly by Segway

Segway rides have restrictions. Riders must be 12 years old or older and weigh between 100-300 pounds (45-135 kg). If you are between 12 and 18 years of age, a parent/guardian must be with you. Other than that – you can ride. Philly by Segway offers a 1-hour or a 2-hour tour of Philadelphia or specialty tours. A couple of choices are a 2-hour Philly Cheesesteak tour, stopping at five of the best cheesesteak joints in Philly, or a 2-hour Mural Tour taking a look at the Philadelphia Murals.

I hope you enjoyed your visit to Philadelphia! Next, let's head south to visit the historical US city of Washington DC where we will learn about US currency and find out about the strange shape of the Washington Monument!

kid-friendly-family-vacations.com/booktour-visitwdc

———————————————————————————————

Signup for my newsletter for all upcoming book updates as well as some cool Philadelphia puzzles and coloring pages!

kid-friendly-family-vacations.com/phillyfun

———————————————————————————————

Visit all the cities in the Hey Kids! Let's Visit series...

kid-friendly-family-vacations.com/series

———————————————————————————————

If you enjoyed your visit to Philadelphia, please leave a review to help others also learn more about Philadelphia whether traveling or learning from home.

kid-friendly-family-vacations.com/review-philly

Also By Teresa Mills and Kid Friendly Family Vacations

Hey Kids! Let's Visit Washington DC

Hey Kids! Let's Visit A Cruise Ship

Hey Kids! Let's Visit New York City

Hey Kids! Let's Visit London England

Hey Kids! Let's Visit San Francisco

Hey Kids! Let's Visit Savannah Georgia

Hey Kids! Let's Visit Paris France

Hey Kids! Let's Visit Charleston South Carolina

Hey Kids! Let's Visit Chicago

Hey Kids! Let's Visit Rome Italy

Hey Kids! Let's Visit Boston

Hey Kids! Let's Visit Philadelphia

Hey Kids! Let's Visit San Diego

Hey Kids! Let's Visit Seattle

Hey Kids! Let's Visit Seoul South Korea

More from Kid Friendly Family Vacations

BOOKS

Books to help build your kids / grandkids life
experiences through travel and learning
https://kid-friendly-family-vacations.com/books

COLORING AND ACTIVITY PAGKAGES

Coloring pages, activity books, printable travel journals,
and more in our Etsy shop
https://kid-friendly-family-vacations.com/etsy

RESOURCES FOR TEACHERS

Resources for teachers on Teachers Pay Teachers
https://kid-friendly-family-vacations.com/tpt

It is our mission to help you build your children's
and grand-children's life experiences through travel.
Not just traveling with your kids... building their Life
Experiences"! Join our community here:
https://kid-friendly-family-vacations.com/join

Acknowledgements

Proofreading / Editing

Katie Erickson – https://www.katieericksonediting.com

Cover Photos

Liberty Bell - © marcorubino / depositphotos.com

Independence Hall - © trekandshoot / depositphotos.com

Love sculpture - © melastmohican / depositphotos.com

cheesesteak - © paulbradyphoto / depositphotos.com

Photos in Book

Independence Visitor Center - © f11photo / depositphotos.com

Liberty Bell - © marcorubino / depositphotos.com

Independence Hall - © trekandshoot / depositphotos.com

Congress Hall - © ReDunnLev / iStockphoto.com

About the Author

Teresa Mills is the bestselling author of the "Hey Kids! Let's Visit..." Book Series for Kids! Teresa's goal through her books and website is to help parents / grandparents who want to build the life experiences of their children / grandchildren through travel and learning activities.

She is an active mother and Mimi. She and her family love traveling in the USA, and internationally too! They love exploring new places, eating cool foods, and having yet another adventure as a family! With the Mills, it's all about traveling as family.

In addition to traveling, Teresa enjoys reading, hiking, biking, and helping others.

Join in the fun at

kid-friendly-family-vacations.com

45602939R00063